THIS BOOK BELONGS TO:

Name: _____

Address: _____

_____

Phone: _____

Email: _____

Sundara Butterfly
Artwork © WR Design Studio

Item #82068

ISBN 978-1-60897-504-4

© Orange Circle Studio Corporation

8687 Research Drive, Suite 150
Irvine, CA 92618
PH 949-727-0800

Calendars • Stationery • Gift Products
www.orangecirclestudio.com

Name:

Address:

Cell: Home:

Work: Other:

Email:

Social Media:

Website / Blog:

Name:

Address:

Cell: Home:

Work: Other:

Email:

Social Media:

Website / Blog:

Name:

Address:

Cell: Home:

Work: Other:

Email:

Social Media:

Website / Blog:

Name: _____

Address: _____

_____

Cell: _____ Home: _____

Work: _____ Other: _____

Email: _____

Social Media: _____

Website / Blog: _____

Name: _____

Address: _____

_____

Cell: _____ Home: _____

Work: _____ Other: _____

Email: _____

Social Media: _____

Website / Blog: _____

Name: _____

Address: _____

_____

Cell: _____ Home: _____

Work: _____ Other: _____

Email: _____

Social Media: _____

Website / Blog: _____

Name:

Address:

Cell: Home:

Work: Other:

Email:

Social Media:

Website / Blog:

Name:

Address:

Cell: Home:

Work: Other:

Email:

Social Media:

Website / Blog:

Name:

Address:

Cell: Home:

Work: Other:

Email:

Social Media:

Website / Blog:

Name:

Address:

Cell: Home:

Work: Other:

Email:

Social Media:

Website / Blog:

Name:

Address:

Cell: Home:

Work: Other:

Email:

Social Media:

Website / Blog:

Name:

Address:

Cell: Home:

Work: Other:

Email:

Social Media:

Website / Blog:

Name:

Address:

Cell: Home:

Work: Other:

Email:

Social Media:

Website / Blog:

Name:

Address:

Cell: Home:

Work: Other:

Email:

Social Media:

Website / Blog:

Name:

Address:

Cell: Home:

Work: Other:

Email:

Social Media:

Website / Blog:

Name:

Address:

Cell: Home:

Work: Other:

Email:

Social Media:

Website / Blog:

Name:

Address:

Cell: Home:

Work: Other:

Email:

Social Media:

Website / Blog:

Name:

Address:

Cell: Home:

Work: Other:

Email:

Social Media:

Website / Blog:

Name:

Address:

Cell: Home:

Work: Other:

Email:

Social Media:

Website / Blog:

Name:

Address:

Cell: Home:

Work: Other:

Email:

Social Media:

Website / Blog:

Name:

Address:

Cell: Home:

Work: Other:

Email:

Social Media:

Website / Blog:

Name:

Address:

Cell: Home:

Work: Other:

Email:

Social Media:

Website / Blog:

Name:

Address:

Cell: Home:

Work: Other:

Email:

Social Media:

Website / Blog:

Name:

Address:

Cell: Home:

Work: Other:

Email:

Social Media:

Website / Blog:

Name:

Address:

Cell: Home:

Work: Other:

Email:

Social Media:

Website / Blog:

Name:

Address:

Cell: Home:

Work: Other:

Email:

Social Media:

Website / Blog:

Name:

Address:

Cell: Home:

Work: Other:

Email:

Social Media:

Website / Blog:

Name:

Address:

Cell: Home:

Work: Other:

Email:

Social Media:

Website / Blog:

Name:

Address:

Cell: Home:

Work: Other:

Email:

Social Media:

Website / Blog:

Name:

Address:

Cell: Home:

Work: Other:

Email:

Social Media:

Website / Blog:

Name:

Address:

Cell: Home:

Work: Other:

Email:

Social Media:

Website / Blog:

Name:

Address:

Cell: Home:

Work: Other:

Email:

Social Media:

Website / Blog:

Name:

Address:

Cell: Home:

Work: Other:

Email:

Social Media:

Website / Blog:

Name:

Address:

Cell: Home:

Work: Other:

Email:

Social Media:

Website / Blog:

Name:

Address:

Cell: Home:

Work: Other:

Email:

Social Media:

Website / Blog:

Name:

Address:

Cell: Home:

Work: Other:

Email:

Social Media:

Website / Blog:

Name:

Address:

Cell: Home:

Work: Other:

Email:

Social Media:

Website / Blog:

Name:

Address:

Cell: Home:

Work: Other:

Email:

Social Media:

Website / Blog:

Name:

Address:

Cell: Home:

Work: Other:

Email:

Social Media:

Website / Blog:

Name:

Address:

Cell: Home:

Work: Other:

Email:

Social Media:

Website / Blog:

Name:

Address:

Cell: Home:

Work: Other:

Email:

Social Media:

Website / Blog:

Name:

Address:

Cell: Home:

Work: Other:

Email:

Social Media:

Website / Blog:

Name:

Address:

Cell: Home:

Work: Other:

Email:

Social Media:

Website / Blog:

Name:

Address:

Cell: Home:

Work: Other:

Email:

Social Media:

Website / Blog:

Name:

Address:

Cell: Home:

Work: Other:

Email:

Social Media:

Website / Blog:

Name: _____

Address: _____

_____

Cell: _____ Home: _____

Work: _____ Other: _____

Email: _____

Social Media: _____

Website / Blog: _____

Name: _____

Address: _____

_____

Cell: _____ Home: _____

Work: _____ Other: _____

Email: _____

Social Media: _____

Website / Blog: _____

Name: _____

Address: _____

_____

Cell: _____ Home: _____

Work: _____ Other: _____

Email: _____

Social Media: _____

Website / Blog: _____

Name:

Address:

Cell: Home:

Work: Other:

Email:

Social Media:

Website / Blog:

Name:

Address:

Cell: Home:

Work: Other:

Email:

Social Media:

Website / Blog:

Name:

Address:

Cell: Home:

Work: Other:

Email:

Social Media:

Website / Blog:

Name: _____

Address: _____

_____

Cell: _____ Home: _____

Work: _____ Other: _____

Email: _____

Social Media: _____

Website / Blog: _____

Name: _____

Address: _____

_____

Cell: _____ Home: _____

Work: _____ Other: _____

Email: _____

Social Media: _____

Website / Blog: _____

Name: _____

Address: _____

_____

Cell: _____ Home: _____

Work: _____ Other: _____

Email: _____

Social Media: _____

Website / Blog: _____

Name:

Address:

Cell: Home:

Work: Other:

Email:

Social Media:

Website / Blog:

Name:

Address:

Cell: Home:

Work: Other:

Email:

Social Media:

Website / Blog:

Name:

Address:

Cell: Home:

Work: Other:

Email:

Social Media:

Website / Blog:

Name:

Address:

Cell: Home:

Work: Other:

Email:

Social Media:

Website / Blog:

Name:

Address:

Cell: Home:

Work: Other:

Email:

Social Media:

Website / Blog:

Name:

Address:

Cell: Home:

Work: Other:

Email:

Social Media:

Website / Blog:

Name:

Address:

Cell: Home:

Work: Other:

Email:

Social Media:

Website / Blog:

Name:

Address:

Cell: Home:

Work: Other:

Email:

Social Media:

Website / Blog:

Name:

Address:

Cell: Home:

Work: Other:

Email:

Social Media:

Website / Blog:

Name:

Address:

Cell: Home:

Work: Other:

Email:

Social Media:

Website / Blog:

Name:

Address:

Cell: Home:

Work: Other:

Email:

Social Media:

Website / Blog:

Name:

Address:

Cell: Home:

Work: Other:

Email:

Social Media:

Website / Blog:

Name:

Address:

Cell: Home:

Work: Other:

Email:

Social Media:

Website / Blog:

Name:

Address:

Cell: Home:

Work: Other:

Email:

Social Media:

Website / Blog:

Name:

Address:

Cell: Home:

Work: Other:

Email:

Social Media:

Website / Blog:

Name:

Address:

Cell: Home:

Work: Other:

Email:

Social Media:

Website / Blog:

Name:

Address:

Cell: Home:

Work: Other:

Email:

Social Media:

Website / Blog:

Name:

Address:

Cell: Home:

Work: Other:

Email:

Social Media:

Website / Blog:

Name:

Address:

Cell: Home:

Work: Other:

Email:

Social Media:

Website / Blog:

Name:

Address:

Cell: Home:

Work: Other:

Email:

Social Media:

Website / Blog:

Name:

Address:

Cell: Home:

Work: Other:

Email:

Social Media:

Website / Blog:

Name:

Address:

Cell: Home:

Work: Other:

Email:

Social Media:

Website / Blog:

Name:

Address:

Cell: Home:

Work: Other:

Email:

Social Media:

Website / Blog:

Name:

Address:

Cell: Home:

Work: Other:

Email:

Social Media:

Website / Blog:

Name:

Address:

Cell: Home:

Work: Other:

Email:

Social Media:

Website / Blog:

Name:

Address:

Cell: Home:

Work: Other:

Email:

Social Media:

Website / Blog:

Name:

Address:

Cell: Home:

Work: Other:

Email:

Social Media:

Website / Blog:

Name: _____

Address: _____

_____

Cell: _____ Home: _____

Work: _____ Other: _____

Email: _____

Social Media: _____

Website / Blog: _____

Name: _____

Address: _____

_____

Cell: _____ Home: _____

Work: _____ Other: _____

Email: _____

Social Media: _____

Website / Blog: _____

Name: _____

Address: _____

_____

Cell: _____ Home: _____

Work: _____ Other: _____

Email: _____

Social Media: _____

Website / Blog: _____

Name:

Address:

Cell: | Home:

Work: | Other:

Email:

Social Media:

Website / Blog:

Name:

Address:

Cell: | Home:

Work: | Other:

Email:

Social Media:

Website / Blog:

Name:

Address:

Cell: | Home:

Work: | Other:

Email:

Social Media:

Website / Blog:

Name:

Address:

Cell: Home:

Work: Other:

Email:

Social Media:

Website / Blog:

Name:

Address:

Cell: Home:

Work: Other:

Email:

Social Media:

Website / Blog:

Name:

Address:

Cell: Home:

Work: Other:

Email:

Social Media:

Website / Blog:

Name:

Address:

Cell: Home:

Work: Other:

Email:

Social Media:

Website / Blog:

Name:

Address:

Cell: Home:

Work: Other:

Email:

Social Media:

Website / Blog:

Name:

Address:

Cell: Home:

Work: Other:

Email:

Social Media:

Website / Blog:

Name:

Address:

Cell: Home:

Work: Other:

Email:

Social Media:

Website / Blog:

Name:

Address:

Cell: Home:

Work: Other:

Email:

Social Media:

Website / Blog:

Name:

Address:

Cell: Home:

Work: Other:

Email:

Social Media:

Website / Blog:

Name:

Address:

Cell: Home:

Work: Other:

Email:

Social Media:

Website / Blog:

Name:

Address:

Cell: Home:

Work: Other:

Email:

Social Media:

Website / Blog:

Name:

Address:

Cell: Home:

Work: Other:

Email:

Social Media:

Website / Blog:

Name:

Address:

Cell: Home:

Work: Other:

Email:

Social Media:

Website / Blog:

Name:

Address:

Cell: Home:

Work: Other:

Email:

Social Media:

Website / Blog:

Name:

Address:

Cell: Home:

Work: Other:

Email:

Social Media:

Website / Blog:

Name:

Address:

Cell: Home:

Work: Other:

Email:

Social Media:

Website / Blog:

Name:

Address:

Cell: Home:

Work: Other:

Email:

Social Media:

Website / Blog:

Name:

Address:

Cell: Home:

Work: Other:

Email:

Social Media:

Website / Blog:

Name:

Address:

Cell: Home:

Work: Other:

Email:

Social Media:

Website / Blog:

Name:

Address:

Cell: Home:

Work: Other:

Email:

Social Media:

Website / Blog:

Name:

Address:

Cell: Home:

Work: Other:

Email:

Social Media:

Website / Blog:

Name:

Address:

Cell: Home:

Work: Other:

Email:

Social Media:

Website / Blog:

Name:

Address:

Cell: Home:

Work: Other:

Email:

Social Media:

Website / Blog:

Name:

Address:

Cell: Home:

Work: Other:

Email:

Social Media:

Website / Blog:

Name:

Address:

Cell: Home:

Work: Other:

Email:

Social Media:

Website / Blog:

Name:

Address:

Cell: Home:

Work: Other:

Email:

Social Media:

Website / Blog:

Name:

Address:

Cell: Home:

Work: Other:

Email:

Social Media:

Website / Blog:

Name:

Address:

Cell: Home:

Work: Other:

Email:

Social Media:

Website / Blog:

Name:

Address:

Cell: Home:

Work: Other:

Email:

Social Media:

Website / Blog:

Name:

Address:

Cell: Home:

Work: Other:

Email:

Social Media:

Website / Blog:

G
H

Name: _____

Address: _____

_____

Cell: _____ Home: _____

Work: _____ Other: _____

Email: _____

Social Media: _____

Website / Blog: _____

Name: _____

Address: _____

_____

Cell: _____ Home: _____

Work: _____ Other: _____

Email: _____

Social Media: _____

Website / Blog: _____

Name: _____

Address: _____

_____

Cell: _____ Home: _____

Work: _____ Other: _____

Email: _____

Social Media: _____

Website / Blog: _____

Name:

Address:

Cell: Home:

Work: Other:

Email:

Social Media:

Website / Blog:

Name:

Address:

Cell: Home:

Work: Other:

Email:

Social Media:

Website / Blog:

Name:

Address:

Cell: Home:

Work: Other:

Email:

Social Media:

Website / Blog:

Name:

Address:

Cell: Home:

Work: Other:

Email:

Social Media:

Website / Blog:

Name:

Address:

Cell: Home:

Work: Other:

Email:

Social Media:

Website / Blog:

Name:

Address:

Cell: Home:

Work: Other:

Email:

Social Media:

Website / Blog:

Name:

Address:

Cell: Home:

Work: Other:

Email:

Social Media:

Website / Blog:

Name:

Address:

Cell: Home:

Work: Other:

Email:

Social Media:

Website / Blog:

Name:

Address:

Cell: Home:

Work: Other:

Email:

Social Media:

Website / Blog:

Name:

Address:

Cell: Home:

Work: Other:

Email:

Social Media:

Website / Blog:

Name:

Address:

Cell: Home:

Work: Other:

Email:

Social Media:

Website / Blog:

Name:

Address:

Cell: Home:

Work: Other:

Email:

Social Media:

Website / Blog:

Name:

Address:

Cell: Home:

Work: Other:

Email:

Social Media:

Website / Blog:

Name:

Address:

Cell: Home:

Work: Other:

Email:

Social Media:

Website / Blog:

Name:

Address:

Cell: Home:

Work: Other:

Email:

Social Media:

Website / Blog:

Name:

Address:

Cell: Home:

Work: Other:

Email:

Social Media:

Website / Blog:

Name:

Address:

Cell: Home:

Work: Other:

Email:

Social Media:

Website / Blog:

Name:

Address:

Cell: Home:

Work: Other:

Email:

Social Media:

Website / Blog:

G
H

Name:

Address:

Cell: Home:

Work: Other:

Email:

Social Media:

Website / Blog:

Name:

Address:

Cell: Home:

Work: Other:

Email:

Social Media:

Website / Blog:

Name:

Address:

Cell: Home:

Work: Other:

Email:

Social Media:

Website / Blog:

Name:

Address:

Cell: Home:

Work: Other:

Email:

Social Media:

Website / Blog:

Name:

Address:

Cell: Home:

Work: Other:

Email:

Social Media:

Website / Blog:

Name:

Address:

Cell: Home:

Work: Other:

Email:

Social Media:

Website / Blog:

Name:

Address:

Cell: Home:

Work: Other:

Email:

Social Media:

Website / Blog:

Name:

Address:

Cell: Home:

Work: Other:

Email:

Social Media:

Website / Blog:

Name:

Address:

Cell: Home:

Work: Other:

Email:

Social Media:

Website / Blog:

Name:

Address:

Cell: Home:

Work: Other:

Email:

Social Media:

Website / Blog:

Name:

Address:

Cell: Home:

Work: Other:

Email:

Social Media:

Website / Blog:

Name:

Address:

Cell: Home:

Work: Other:

Email:

Social Media:

Website / Blog:

Name:

Address:

Cell: Home:

Work: Other:

Email:

Social Media:

Website / Blog:

Name:

Address:

Cell: Home:

Work: Other:

Email:

Social Media:

Website / Blog:

Name:

Address:

Cell: Home:

Work: Other:

Email:

Social Media:

Website / Blog:

Name:

Address:

Cell: Home:

Work: Other:

Email:

Social Media:

Website / Blog:

Name:

Address:

Cell: Home:

Work: Other:

Email:

Social Media:

Website / Blog:

Name:

Address:

Cell: Home:

Work: Other:

Email:

Social Media:

Website / Blog:

Name:

Address:

Cell: Home:

Work: Other:

Email:

Social Media:

Website / Blog:

Name:

Address:

Cell: Home:

Work: Other:

Email:

Social Media:

Website / Blog:

Name:

Address:

Cell: Home:

Work: Other:

Email:

Social Media:

Website / Blog:

Name:

Address:

Cell: Home:

Work: Other:

Email:

Social Media:

Website / Blog:

Name:

Address:

Cell: Home:

Work: Other:

Email:

Social Media:

Website / Blog:

Name:

Address:

Cell: Home:

Work: Other:

Email:

Social Media:

Website / Blog:

Name:

Address:

Cell: Home:

Work: Other:

Email:

Social Media:

Website / Blog:

Name:

Address:

Cell: Home:

Work: Other:

Email:

Social Media:

Website / Blog:

Name:

Address:

Cell: Home:

Work: Other:

Email:

Social Media:

Website / Blog:

Name:

Address:

Cell: Home:

Work: Other:

Email:

Social Media:

Website / Blog:

Name:

Address:

Cell: Home:

Work: Other:

Email:

Social Media:

Website / Blog:

Name:

Address:

Cell: Home:

Work: Other:

Email:

Social Media:

Website / Blog:

Name:

Address:

Cell: Home:

Work: Other:

Email:

Social Media:

Website / Blog:

Name:

Address:

Cell: Home:

Work: Other:

Email:

Social Media:

Website / Blog:

Name:

Address:

Cell: Home:

Work: Other:

Email:

Social Media:

Website / Blog:

Name:

Address:

Cell: Home:

Work: Other:

Email:

Social Media:

Website / Blog:

Name:

Address:

Cell: Home:

Work: Other:

Email:

Social Media:

Website / Blog:

Name:

Address:

Cell: Home:

Work: Other:

Email:

Social Media:

Website / Blog:

Name:

Address:

Cell: Home:

Work: Other:

Email:

Social Media:

Website / Blog:

Name:

Address:

Cell: Home:

Work: Other:

Email:

Social Media:

Website / Blog:

Name:

Address:

Cell: Home:

Work: Other:

Email:

Social Media:

Website / Blog:

Name:

Address:

Cell: Home:

Work: Other:

Email:

Social Media:

Website / Blog:

Name:

Address:

Cell: Home:

Work: Other:

Email:

Social Media:

Website / Blog:

Name:

Address:

Cell: Home:

Work: Other:

Email:

Social Media:

Website / Blog:

Name:

Address:

Cell: Home:

Work: Other:

Email:

Social Media:

Website / Blog:

Name:

Address:

Cell: Home:

Work: Other:

Email:

Social Media:

Website / Blog:

Name:

Address:

Cell: Home:

Work: Other:

Email:

Social Media:

Website / Blog:

Name:

Address:

Cell: Home:

Work: Other:

Email:

Social Media:

Website / Blog:

Name:

Address:

Cell: Home:

Work: Other:

Email:

Social Media:

Website / Blog:

Name:

Address:

Cell: Home:

Work: Other:

Email:

Social Media:

Website / Blog:

Name:

Address:

Cell: Home:

Work: Other:

Email:

Social Media:

Website / Blog:

Name:

Address:

Cell: Home:

Work: Other:

Email:

Social Media:

Website / Blog:

Name:

Address:

Cell: Home:

Work: Other:

Email:

Social Media:

Website / Blog:

Name:

Address:

Cell: Home:

Work: Other:

Email:

Social Media:

Website / Blog:

Name:

Address:

Cell: Home:

Work: Other:

Email:

Social Media:

Website / Blog:

Name:

Address:

Cell: Home:

Work: Other:

Email:

Social Media:

Website / Blog:

Name:

Address:

Cell: Home:

Work: Other:

Email:

Social Media:

Website / Blog:

Name:

Address:

Cell: Home:

Work: Other:

Email:

Social Media:

Website / Blog:

Name:

Address:

Cell: Home:

Work: Other:

Email:

Social Media:

Website / Blog:

Name:

Address:

Cell: | Home:

Work: | Other:

Email:

Social Media:

Website / Blog:

Name:

Address:

Cell: | Home:

Work: | Other:

Email:

Social Media:

Website / Blog:

Name:

Address:

Cell: | Home:

Work: | Other:

Email:

Social Media:

Website / Blog:

Name:

Address:

Cell: Home:

Work: Other:

Email:

Social Media:

Website / Blog:

Name:

Address:

Cell: Home:

Work: Other:

Email:

Social Media:

Website / Blog:

Name:

Address:

Cell: Home:

Work: Other:

Email:

Social Media:

Website / Blog:

Name:

Address:

Cell: Home:

Work: Other:

Email:

Social Media:

Website / Blog:

Name:

Address:

Cell: Home:

Work: Other:

Email:

Social Media:

Website / Blog:

Name:

Address:

Cell: Home:

Work: Other:

Email:

Social Media:

Website / Blog:

Name:

Address:

Cell: Home:

Work: Other:

Email:

Social Media:

Website / Blog:

Name:

Address:

Cell: Home:

Work: Other:

Email:

Social Media:

Website / Blog:

Name:

Address:

Cell: Home:

Work: Other:

Email:

Social Media:

Website / Blog:

Name:

Address:

Cell: Home:

Work: Other:

Email:

Social Media:

Website / Blog:

Name:

Address:

Cell: Home:

Work: Other:

Email:

Social Media:

Website / Blog:

Name:

Address:

Cell: Home:

Work: Other:

Email:

Social Media:

Website / Blog:

M
N

Name:

Address:

Cell: Home:

Work: Other:

Email:

Social Media:

Website / Blog:

Name:

Address:

Cell: Home:

Work: Other:

Email:

Social Media:

Website / Blog:

Name:

Address:

Cell: Home:

Work: Other:

Email:

Social Media:

Website / Blog:

Name:

Address:

Cell: Home:

Work: Other:

Email:

Social Media:

Website / Blog:

Name:

Address:

Cell: Home:

Work: Other:

Email:

Social Media:

Website / Blog:

Name:

Address:

Cell: Home:

Work: Other:

Email:

Social Media:

Website / Blog:

Name:

Address:

Cell: Home:

Work: Other:

Email:

Social Media:

Website / Blog:

Name:

Address:

Cell: Home:

Work: Other:

Email:

Social Media:

Website / Blog:

Name:

Address:

Cell: Home:

Work: Other:

Email:

Social Media:

Website / Blog:

M
N

Name: _____

Address: _____

_____

Cell: _____ Home: _____

Work: _____ Other: _____

Email: _____

Social Media: _____

Website / Blog: _____

Name: _____

Address: _____

_____

Cell: _____ Home: _____

Work: _____ Other: _____

Email: _____

Social Media: _____

Website / Blog: _____

Name: _____

Address: _____

_____

Cell: _____ Home: _____

Work: _____ Other: _____

Email: _____

Social Media: _____

Website / Blog: _____

M
N

Name:

Address:

Cell: Home:

Work: Other:

Email:

Social Media:

Website / Blog:

Name:

Address:

Cell: Home:

Work: Other:

Email:

Social Media:

Website / Blog:

Name:

Address:

Cell: Home:

Work: Other:

Email:

Social Media:

Website / Blog:

M
N

Name:

Address:

Cell: Home:

Work: Other:

Email:

Social Media:

Website / Blog:

Name:

Address:

Cell: Home:

Work: Other:

Email:

Social Media:

Website / Blog:

Name:

Address:

Cell: Home:

Work: Other:

Email:

Social Media:

Website / Blog:

M
N

Name:

Address:

Cell: Home:

Work: Other:

Email:

Social Media:

Website / Blog:

Name:

Address:

Cell: Home:

Work: Other:

Email:

Social Media:

Website / Blog:

Name:

Address:

Cell: Home:

Work: Other:

Email:

Social Media:

Website / Blog:

M
N

Name:

Address:

Cell: Home:

Work: Other:

Email:

Social Media:

Website / Blog:

Name:

Address:

Cell: Home:

Work: Other:

Email:

Social Media:

Website / Blog:

Name:

Address:

Cell: Home:

Work: Other:

Email:

Social Media:

Website / Blog:

Name:

Address:

Cell: Home:

Work: Other:

Email:

Social Media:

Website / Blog:

Name:

Address:

Cell: Home:

Work: Other:

Email:

Social Media:

Website / Blog:

Name:

Address:

Cell: Home:

Work: Other:

Email:

Social Media:

Website / Blog:

Name:

Address:

Cell: Home:

Work: Other:

Email:

Social Media:

Website / Blog:

Name:

Address:

Cell: Home:

Work: Other:

Email:

Social Media:

Website / Blog:

Name:

Address:

Cell: Home:

Work: Other:

Email:

Social Media:

Website / Blog:

Name:

Address:

Cell: Home:

Work: Other:

Email:

Social Media:

Website / Blog:

Name:

Address:

Cell: Home:

Work: Other:

Email:

Social Media:

Website / Blog:

Name:

Address:

Cell: Home:

Work: Other:

Email:

Social Media:

Website / Blog:

M
N

Name:

Address:

Cell: Home:

Work: Other:

Email:

Social Media:

Website / Blog:

Name:

Address:

Cell: Home:

Work: Other:

Email:

Social Media:

Website / Blog:

Name:

Address:

Cell: Home:

Work: Other:

Email:

Social Media:

Website / Blog:

Name:

Address:

Cell: Home:

Work: Other:

Email:

Social Media:

Website / Blog:

Name:

Address:

Cell: Home:

Work: Other:

Email:

Social Media:

Website / Blog:

Name:

Address:

Cell: Home:

Work: Other:

Email:

Social Media:

Website / Blog:

O
P

Name:

Address:

Cell: Home:

Work: Other:

Email:

Social Media:

Website / Blog:

Name:

Address:

Cell: Home:

Work: Other:

Email:

Social Media:

Website / Blog:

Name:

Address:

Cell: Home:

Work: Other:

Email:

Social Media:

Website / Blog:

Name:

Address:

Cell: Home:

Work: Other:

Email:

Social Media:

Website / Blog:

Name:

Address:

Cell: Home:

Work: Other:

Email:

Social Media:

Website / Blog:

Name:

Address:

Cell: Home:

Work: Other:

Email:

Social Media:

Website / Blog:

Name:

Address:

Cell: Home:

Work: Other:

Email:

Social Media:

Website / Blog:

Name:

Address:

Cell: Home:

Work: Other:

Email:

Social Media:

Website / Blog:

Name:

Address:

Cell: Home:

Work: Other:

Email:

Social Media:

Website / Blog:

Name:

Address:

Cell: Home:

Work: Other:

Email:

Social Media:

Website / Blog:

Name:

Address:

Cell: Home:

Work: Other:

Email:

Social Media:

Website / Blog:

Name:

Address:

Cell: Home:

Work: Other:

Email:

Social Media:

Website / Blog:

Name:

Address:

Cell: Home:

Work: Other:

Email:

Social Media:

Website / Blog:

Name:

Address:

Cell: Home:

Work: Other:

Email:

Social Media:

Website / Blog:

Name:

Address:

Cell: Home:

Work: Other:

Email:

Social Media:

Website / Blog:

Name:

Address:

Cell: Home:

Work: Other:

Email:

Social Media:

Website / Blog:

Name:

Address:

Cell: Home:

Work: Other:

Email:

Social Media:

Website / Blog:

Name:

Address:

Cell: Home:

Work: Other:

Email:

Social Media:

Website / Blog:

Name:

Address:

Cell: Home:

Work: Other:

Email:

Social Media:

Website / Blog:

Name:

Address:

Cell: Home:

Work: Other:

Email:

Social Media:

Website / Blog:

Name:

Address:

Cell: Home:

Work: Other:

Email:

Social Media:

Website / Blog:

Name:

Address:

Cell: Home:

Work: Other:

Email:

Social Media:

Website / Blog:

Name:

Address:

Cell: Home:

Work: Other:

Email:

Social Media:

Website / Blog:

Name:

Address:

Cell: Home:

Work: Other:

Email:

Social Media:

Website / Blog:

Name:

Address:

Cell: Home:

Work: Other:

Email: .

Social Media:

Website / Blog:

Name:

Address:

Cell: Home:

Work: Other:

Email:

Social Media:

Website / Blog:

Name:

Address:

Cell: Home:

Work: Other:

Email:

Social Media:

Website / Blog:

Name:

Address:

Cell: Home:

Work: Other:

Email:

Social Media:

Website / Blog:

Name:

Address:

Cell: Home:

Work: Other:

Email:

Social Media:

Website / Blog:

Name:

Address:

Cell: Home:

Work: Other:

Email:

Social Media:

Website / Blog:

O
P

O P

Name:
_____

Address:
_____

_____

Cell: _____ Home: _____

Work: _____ Other: _____

Email:
_____

Social Media:
_____

Website / Blog:
_____

Name:
_____

Address:
_____

_____

Cell: _____ Home: _____

Work: _____ Other: _____

Email:
_____

Social Media:
_____

Website / Blog:
_____

Name:
_____

Address:
_____

_____

Cell: _____ Home: _____

Work: _____ Other: _____

Email:
_____

Social Media:
_____

Website / Blog:
_____

Name:

Address:

Cell: Home:

Work: Other:

Email:

Social Media:

Website / Blog:

Name:

Address:

Cell: Home:

Work: Other:

Email:

Social Media:

Website / Blog:

Name:

Address:

Cell: Home:

Work: Other:

Email:

Social Media:

Website / Blog:

Q R

Name:

Address:

Cell: Home:

Work: Other:

Email:

Social Media:

Website / Blog:

Name:

Address:

Cell: Home:

Work: Other:

Email:

Social Media:

Website / Blog:

Name:

Address:

Cell: Home:

Work: Other:

Email:

Social Media:

Website / Blog:

Name:

Address:

Cell: Home:

Work: Other:

Email:

Social Media:

Website / Blog:

Name:

Address:

Cell: Home:

Work: Other:

Email:

Social Media:

Website / Blog:

Name:

Address:

Cell: Home:

Work: Other:

Email:

Social Media:

Website / Blog:

Name:

Address:

Cell: Home:

Work: Other:

Email:

Social Media:

Website / Blog:

Name:

Address:

Cell: Home:

Work: Other:

Email:

Social Media:

Website / Blog:

Name:

Address:

Cell: Home:

Work: Other:

Email:

Social Media:

Website / Blog:

Q
R

Name:

Address:

Cell: Home:

Work: Other:

Email:

Social Media:

Website / Blog:

Name:

Address:

Cell: Home:

Work: Other:

Email:

Social Media:

Website / Blog:

Name:

Address:

Cell: Home:

Work: Other:

Email:

Social Media:

Website / Blog:

Q R

Name:

Address:

Cell: Home:

Work: Other:

Email:

Social Media:

Website / Blog:

Name:

Address:

Cell: Home:

Work: Other:

Email:

Social Media:

Website / Blog:

Name:

Address:

Cell: Home:

Work: Other:

Email:

Social Media:

Website / Blog:

Name:

Address:

Cell: Home:

Work: Other:

Email:

Social Media:

Website / Blog:

Name:

Address:

Cell: Home:

Work: Other:

Email:

Social Media:

Website / Blog:

Name:

Address:

Cell: Home:

Work: Other:

Email:

Social Media:

Website / Blog:

Q R

Name:

Address:

Cell: Home:

Work: Other:

Email:

Social Media:

Website / Blog:

Name:

Address:

Cell: Home:

Work: Other:

Email:

Social Media:

Website / Blog:

Name:

Address:

Cell: Home:

Work: Other:

Email:

Social Media:

Website / Blog:

Name:

Address:

Cell: Home:

Work: Other:

Email:

Social Media:

Website / Blog:

Name:

Address:

Cell: Home:

Work: Other:

Email:

Social Media:

Website / Blog:

Name:

Address:

Cell: Home:

Work: Other:

Email:

Social Media:

Website / Blog:

Name:

Address:

Cell: Home:

Work: Other:

Email:

Social Media:

Website / Blog:

Name:

Address:

Cell: Home:

Work: Other:

Email:

Social Media:

Website / Blog:

Name:

Address:

Cell: Home:

Work: Other:

Email:

Social Media:

Website / Blog:

Name:

Address:

Cell: Home:

Work: Other:

Email:

Social Media:

Website / Blog:

Name:

Address:

Cell: Home:

Work: Other:

Email:

Social Media:

Website / Blog:

Name:

Address:

Cell: Home:

Work: Other:

Email:

Social Media:

Website / Blog:

Q R

Name:

Address:

Cell: Home:

Work: Other:

Email:

Social Media:

Website / Blog:

Name:

Address:

Cell: Home:

Work: Other:

Email:

Social Media:

Website / Blog:

Name:

Address:

Cell: Home:

Work: Other:

Email:

Social Media:

Website / Blog:

Name:

Address:

Cell: Home:

Work: Other:

Email:

Social Media:

Website / Blog:

Name:

Address:

Cell: Home:

Work: Other:

Email:

Social Media:

Website / Blog:

Name:

Address:

Cell: Home:

Work: Other:

Email:

Social Media:

Website / Blog:

Name:

Address:

Cell: Home:

Work: Other:

Email:

Social Media:

Website / Blog:

Name:

Address:

Cell: Home:

Work: Other:

Email:

Social Media:

Website / Blog:

Name:

Address:

Cell: Home:

Work: Other:

Email:

Social Media:

Website / Blog:

Name:

Address:

Cell: Home:

Work: Other:

Email:

Social Media:

Website / Blog:

Name:

Address:

Cell: Home:

Work: Other:

Email:

Social Media:

Website / Blog:

Name:

Address:

Cell: Home:

Work: Other:

Email:

Social Media:

Website / Blog:

Name:

Address:

Cell: Home:

Work: Other:

Email:

Social Media:

Website / Blog:

Name:

Address:

Cell: Home:

Work: Other:

Email:

Social Media:

Website / Blog:

Name:

Address:

Cell: Home:

Work: Other:

Email:

Social Media:

Website / Blog:

Name:

Address:

Cell: Home:

Work: Other:

Email:

Social Media:

Website / Blog:

Name:

Address:

Cell: Home:

Work: Other:

Email:

Social Media:

Website / Blog:

Name:

Address:

Cell: Home:

Work: Other:

Email:

Social Media:

Website / Blog:

Name:

Address:

Cell: Home:

Work: Other:

Email:

Social Media:

Website / Blog:

Name:

Address:

Cell: Home:

Work: Other:

Email:

Social Media:

Website / Blog:

Name:

Address:

Cell: Home:

Work: Other:

Email:

Social Media:

Website / Blog:

Name:

Address:

Cell: Home:

Work: Other:

Email:

Social Media:

Website / Blog:

Name:

Address:

Cell: Home:

Work: Other:

Email:

Social Media:

Website / Blog:

Name:

Address:

Cell: Home:

Work: Other:

Email:

Social Media:

Website / Blog:

Name:

Address:

Cell: Home:

Work: Other:

Email:

Social Media:

Website / Blog:

Name:

Address:

Cell: Home:

Work: Other:

Email:

Social Media:

Website / Blog:

Name:

Address:

Cell: Home:

Work: Other:

Email:

Social Media:

Website / Blog:

**S
T**

Name:

Address:

Cell: Home:

Work: Other:

Email:

Social Media:

Website / Blog:

Name:

Address:

Cell: Home:

Work: Other:

Email:

Social Media:

Website / Blog:

Name:

Address:

Cell: Home:

Work: Other:

Email:

Social Media:

Website / Blog:

Name:

Address:

Cell: Home:

Work: Other:

Email:

Social Media:

Website / Blog:

Name:

Address:

Cell: Home:

Work: Other:

Email:

Social Media:

Website / Blog:

Name:

Address:

Cell: Home:

Work: Other:

Email:

Social Media:

Website / Blog:

S
T

Name:

Address:

Cell: Home:

Work: Other:

Email:

Social Media:

Website / Blog:

Name:

Address:

Cell: Home:

Work: Other:

Email:

Social Media:

Website / Blog:

Name:

Address:

Cell: Home:

Work: Other:

Email:

Social Media:

Website / Blog:

Name:

Address:

Cell: Home:

Work: Other:

Email:

Social Media:

Website / Blog:

Name:

Address:

Cell: Home:

Work: Other:

Email:

Social Media:

Website / Blog:

Name:

Address:

Cell: Home:

Work: Other:

Email:

Social Media:

Website / Blog:

S
T

Name:

Address:

Cell: Home:

Work: Other:

Email:

Social Media:

Website / Blog:

Name:

Address:

Cell: Home:

Work: Other:

Email:

Social Media:

Website / Blog:

Name:

Address:

Cell: Home:

Work: Other:

Email:

Social Media:

Website / Blog:

Name:

Address:

Cell: Home:

Work: Other:

Email:

Social Media:

Website / Blog:

Name:

Address:

Cell: Home:

Work: Other:

Email:

Social Media:

Website / Blog:

Name:

Address:

Cell: Home:

Work: Other:

Email:

Social Media:

Website / Blog:

Name:

Address:

Cell: Home:

Work: Other:

Email:

Social Media:

Website / Blog:

Name:

Address:

Cell: Home:

Work: Other:

Email:

Social Media:

Website / Blog:

Name:

Address:

Cell: Home:

Work: Other:

Email:

Social Media:

Website / Blog:

Name:

Address:

Cell: Home:

Work: Other:

Email:

Social Media:

Website / Blog:

Name:

Address:

Cell: Home:

Work: Other:

Email:

Social Media:

Website / Blog:

Name:

Address:

Cell: Home:

Work: Other:

Email:

Social Media:

Website / Blog:

Name:

Address:

Cell: Home:

Work: Other:

Email:

Social Media:

Website / Blog:

Name:

Address:

Cell: Home:

Work: Other:

Email:

Social Media:

Website / Blog:

Name:

Address:

Cell: Home:

Work: Other:

Email:

Social Media:

Website / Blog:

Name:

Address:

Cell: Home:

Work: Other:

Email:

Social Media:

Website / Blog:

Name:

Address:

Cell: Home:

Work: Other:

Email:

Social Media:

Website / Blog:

Name:

Address:

Cell: Home:

Work: Other:

Email:

Social Media:

Website / Blog:

Name:

Address:

Cell: Home:

Work: Other:

Email:

Social Media:

Website / Blog:

Name:

Address:

Cell: Home:

Work: Other:

Email:

Social Media:

Website / Blog:

Name:

Address:

Cell: Home:

Work: Other:

Email:

Social Media:

Website / Blog:

Name:

Address:

Cell: Home:

Work: Other:

Email:

Social Media:

Website / Blog:

Name:

Address:

Cell: Home:

Work: Other:

Email:

Social Media:

Website / Blog:

Name:

Address:

Cell: Home:

Work: Other:

Email:

Social Media:

Website / Blog:

Name:

Address:

Cell: Home:

Work: Other:

Email:

Social Media:

Website / Blog:

Name:

Address:

Cell: Home:

Work: Other:

Email:

Social Media:

Website / Blog:

Name:

Address:

Cell: Home:

Work: Other:

Email:

Social Media:

Website / Blog:

Name:

Address:

Cell: Home:

Work: Other:

Email:

Social Media:

Website / Blog:

Name:

Address:

Cell: Home:

Work: Other:

Email:

Social Media:

Website / Blog:

Name:

Address:

Cell: Home:

Work: Other:

Email:

Social Media:

Website / Blog:

Name:

Address:

Cell: Home:

Work: Other:

Email:

Social Media:

Website / Blog:

Name:

Address:

Cell: Home:

Work: Other:

Email:

Social Media:

Website / Blog:

Name:

Address:

Cell: Home:

Work: Other:

Email:

Social Media:

Website / Blog:

Name:

Address:

Cell: Home:

Work: Other:

Email:

Social Media:

Website / Blog:

Name:

Address:

Cell: Home:

Work: Other:

Email:

Social Media:

Website / Blog:

Name:

Address:

Cell: Home:

Work: Other:

Email:

Social Media:

Website / Blog:

Name:

Address:

Cell: Home:

Work: Other:

Email:

Social Media:

Website / Blog:

Name:

Address:

Cell: Home:

Work: Other:

Email:

Social Media:

Website / Blog:

Name:

Address:

Cell: Home:

Work: Other:

Email:

Social Media:

Website / Blog:

X
Y
Z

Name:

Address:

Cell: Home:

Work: Other:

Email:

Social Media:

Website / Blog:

Name:

Address:

Cell: Home:

Work: Other:

Email:

Social Media:

Website / Blog:

Name:

Address:

Cell: Home:

Work: Other:

Email:

Social Media:

Website / Blog:

X
Y
Z

Name:

Address:

Cell: Home:

Work: Other:

Email:

Social Media:

Website / Blog:

Name:

Address:

Cell: Home:

Work: Other:

Email:

Social Media:

Website / Blog:

Name:

Address:

Cell: Home:

Work: Other:

Email:

Social Media:

Website / Blog:

Name: _____

Address: _____

_____

Cell: _____ Home: _____

Work: _____ Other: _____

Email: _____

Social Media: _____

Website / Blog: _____

Name: _____

Address: _____

_____

Cell: _____ Home: _____

Work: _____ Other: _____

Email: _____

Social Media: _____

Website / Blog: _____

Name: _____

Address: _____

_____

Cell: _____ Home: _____

Work: _____ Other: _____

Email: _____

Social Media: _____

Website / Blog: _____

Name:

Address:

Cell: Home:

Work: Other:

Email:

Social Media:

Website / Blog:

Name:

Address:

Cell: Home:

Work: Other:

Email:

Social Media:

Website / Blog:

Name:

Address:

Cell: Home:

Work: Other:

Email:

Social Media:

Website / Blog:

Name:

Address:

Cell: Home:

Work: Other:

Email:

Social Media:

Website / Blog:

Name:

Address:

Cell: Home:

Work: Other:

Email:

Social Media:

Website / Blog:

Name:

Address:

Cell: Home:

Work: Other:

Email:

Social Media:

Website / Blog:

Name:

Address:

Cell: Home:

Work: Other:

Email:

Social Media:

Website / Blog:

Name:

Address:

Cell: Home:

Work: Other:

Email:

Social Media:

Website / Blog:

Name:

Address:

Cell: Home:

Work: Other:

Email:

Social Media:

Website / Blog:

Name: _____

Address: _____

_____

Cell: _____ Home: _____

Work: _____ Other: _____

Email: _____

Social Media: _____

Website / Blog: _____

Name: _____

Address: _____

_____

Cell: _____ Home: _____

Work: _____ Other: _____

Email: _____

Social Media: _____

Website / Blog: _____

Name: _____

Address: _____

_____

Cell: _____ Home: _____

Work: _____ Other: _____

Email: _____

Social Media: _____

Website / Blog: _____

Name:

Address:

Cell: Home:

Work: Other:

Email:

Social Media:

Website / Blog:

Name:

Address:

Cell: Home:

Work: Other:

Email:

Social Media:

Website / Blog:

Name:

Address:

Cell: Home:

Work: Other:

Email:

Social Media:

Website / Blog:

Name:

Address:

Cell: Home:

Work: Other:

Email:

Social Media:

Website / Blog:

Name:

Address:

Cell: Home:

Work: Other:

Email:

Social Media:

Website / Blog:

Name:

Address:

Cell: Home:

Work: Other:

Email:

Social Media:

Website / Blog:

Name:

Address:

Cell: Home:

Work: Other:

Email:

Social Media:

Website / Blog:

Name:

Address:

Cell: Home:

Work: Other:

Email:

Social Media:

Website / Blog:

Name:

Address:

Cell: Home:

Work: Other:

Email:

Social Media:

Website / Blog:

Name:

Address:

Cell: Home:

Work: Other:

Email:

Social Media:

Website / Blog:

Name:

Address:

Cell: Home:

Work: Other:

Email:

Social Media:

Website / Blog:

Name:

Address:

Cell: Home:

Work: Other:

Email:

Social Media:

Website / Blog:

Website:

URL:

Username:

Password:

Notes:

Website:

URL:

Username:

Password:

Notes:

Website:

URL:

Username:

Password:

Notes:

PASSWORDS

Website:

URL:

Username:

Password:

Notes:

Website:

URL:

Username:

Password:

Notes:

Website:

URL:

Username:

Password:

Notes:

bsite:

RL:

ername:

ssword:

tes:

---

bsite:

.L:

ername:

sword:

tes:

---

bsite:

L:

ername:

sword:

es:

PASSWORDS

Website:

URL:

Username:

Password:

Notes:

Website:

URL:

Username:

Password:

Notes:

Website:

URL:

Username:

Password:

Notes:

Website:

URL:

Username:

Password:

Notes:

Website:

URL:

Username:

Password:

Notes:

Website:

URL:

Username:

Password:

Notes:

PASSWORDS

Website:

URL:

Username:

Password:

Notes:

Website:

URL:

Username:

Password:

Notes:

Website:

URL:

Username:

Password:

Notes:

Website:

URL:

Username:

Password:

Notes:

Website:

URL:

Username:

Password:

Notes:

Website:

URL:

Username:

Password:

Notes:

PASSWORDS

Website:

URL:

Username:

Password:

Notes:

Website:

URL:

Username:

Password:

Notes:

Website:

URL:

Username:

Password:

Notes:

Website: _____

URL: _____

Username: _____

Password: _____

Notes: _____

_____

_____

Website: _____

URL: _____

Username: _____

Password: _____

Notes: _____

_____

_____

Website: _____

URL: _____

Username: _____

Password: _____

Notes: _____

_____

_____

PASSWORDS

Website:

URL:

Username:

Password:

Notes:

Website:

URL:

Username:

Password:

Notes:

Website:

URL:

Username:

Password:

Notes:

Website: _____

URL: _____

Username: _____

Password: _____

Notes: _____

_____

_____

Website: _____

URL: _____

Username: _____

Password: _____

Notes: _____

_____

_____

Website: _____

URL: _____

Username: _____

Password: _____

Notes: _____

_____

_____

PASSWORDS

Website:

URL:

Username:

Password:

Notes:

Website:

URL:

Username:

Password:

Notes:

Website:

URL:

Username:

Password:

Notes:

Name:

Address:

Cell:

Work: Home:

Email: Other:

Social Media:

Website / Blog:

Name:

Address:

Cell:

Work: Home:

Email: Other:

Social Media:

Website / Blog:

Name:

Address:

Cell:

Work: Home:

Email: Other:

Social Media:

Website / Blog:

Name:

Address:

Cell:

Work: Home:

Email: Other:

Social Media:

Website / Blog:

Name:

Address:

Cell:

Work: Home:

Email: Other:

Social Media:

Website / Blog:

Name:

Address:

Cell:

Work: Home:

Email: Other:

Social Media:

Website / Blog:

Name:

Address:

Cell:

Work: Home:

Email: Other:

Social Media:

Website / Blog:

Name:

Address:

Cell:

Work: Home:

Email: Other:

Social Media:

Website / Blog:

Name:

Address:

Cell:

Work: Home:

Email: Other:

Social Media:

Website / Blog:

Name:

Address:

Cell:

Work: Home:

Email: Other:

Social Media:

Website / Blog:

Name:

Address:

Cell:

Work: Home:

Email: Other:

Social Media:

Website / Blog:

Name:

Address:

Cell:

Work: Home:

Email: Other:

Social Media:

Website / Blog: